. . . if we write but one book in life,
let it be our autobiography.

TIMEPIECE

Designed by Jed N. Platt
Author Illustration by Laura E. Harris

Manufactured in The United States of America

3 5 7 9 10 8 6 4 2

Distributed by Evans Book
(801) 975-1315

ISBN 1-56684-580-7

The Quotable Evans

A collection of Diary Entries, Letters and Lessons

from the first five novels of

RICHARD PAUL EVANS

ABOUT RICHARD PAUL EVANS

Richard Paul Evans was born in 1962 in Salt Lake City, Utah, the seventh of eight children. He did not aspire to be a published writer. His first novel, *The Christmas Box,* was a story he wrote for his two young daughters. At the encouragement of family and friends he self-published the book. It became a #1 international bestseller. He is the president and founder of The Christmas Box Charitable Foundation, which supports several humanitarian projects for children throughout the world. Richard currently lives in Salt Lake City with his wife Keri and their five children.

Contents

PROLOGUE

DIARIES AND LETTERS

LIFE'S LESSONS

$\mathscr{P}$ROLOGUE

I was speaking to an audience in a bookstore about my latest novel when a woman raised her hand with a question.

"Do you ever intend to publish David Parkin's Diary?"

The question caught me off guard. "His diary? There is no diary."

She said, without hesitation, "The diary you quote from in your books."

The audience laughed.

"David Parkin is a fictitious character," I explained. "There is no diary."

"Then who wrote the diary entries in your book?" she asked.

"I wrote them."

She looked bewildered. "You wrote them?"

I nodded. "Yes, ma'am."

The woman thought about it for a moment then said, "I don't mean to insult you, Mr. Evans, but I think David Parkin is a better writer than you are."

Many of my readers, in their letters and at book signings, have told me that their favorite part of my books are the diary entries that precede each chapter. I started the diary entries for the simple reason that I could not decide whether to write my second novel, *Timepiece,* in first person or third. I decided to do both; to write third person and use the diary entries to show David Parkin's thoughts.

Because of the response I received from my readers, I have included the diary entries with each successive novel. It has become a trademark of my writing.

I hope you enjoy this collection of favorite passages and thoughts, and, when occasion permits, share them with others.

With warm regards,
Richard Paul Evans

Diaries and Letters

The Christmas Box

I have learned from those who have read my stories that books can heal, and characters like MaryAnne Parkin, though fictitious, can provide warmth, companionship and insight to our own lives.

December 6, 1920

My Beloved One,

How I wish that I might say these things to your gentle face and that this box may be found empty. Even as the mother of our Lord found the tomb they placed Him in empty. And in this, there is hope, my love. Hope of embracing you again and holding you to my breast. And this because of the great gift of Christmas. Because He came. The first Christmas offering from a parent to His children, because He loved them and wanted them back. I understand that in ways I never understood before, as my love for you has not waned with time, but has grown brighter with each Christmas season. How I look forward to that glorious day that I hold you again. I love you, my little angel.

Mother

Timepiece

Timepiece *is a story of love, loss and forgiveness. The diary entries in this novel follow this pattern, from the early romance of David and MaryAnne Parkin, to the loss of their little girl. Not surprisingly, many of the quotes are about time—and our place in it.*

"The first mechanical clock was invented in the year A.D. 979 in Kaifeng, China. Commissioned by the boy emperor for the purpose of astrological fortunetelling, the clock took eight years to construct and weighed more than two tons. Though of monstrous dimensions, the device was remarkably efficient, striking a gong every fourteen minutes and twenty-four seconds, nearly identical to our modern-day standard, at the same time turning massive rings designed to replicate the celestial movements of the three luminaries: the sun, the moon, and selected stars, all of which were crucial to Chinese astrological divination.

"When the Tartars invaded China in 1108, they plundered the capital city and after disassembling the massive clock, carted it back to their own lands. Unable to put the precision piece back together, they melted it down for swords."

NOTE IN DAVID PARKIN'S DIARY

15

"Of all, clockmakers and morticians should bear the keenest sense of priority—their lives daily spent in observance of the unflagging procession of time...and the end thereof."

DAVID PARKIN'S DIARY. JANUARY 3, 1901

✺

"A conspiracy of florists, caterers, and clergy have done too well a job of shrouding the virtues of the elopement."

DAVID PARKIN'S DIARY. JULY 5, 1908

✺

"If the heavens were to open and a host of Angels descend, they could not have produced such an effect on my soul as MaryAnne descending the chapel staircase for our wedding."

DAVID PARKIN'S DIARY. AUGUST 11, 1908

✺

"I had never supposed the cost women bear in the perpetuation of the species. Nor that such courage could be had in such a petite frame."

DAVID PARKIN'S DIARY. JANUARY 17, 1909

❋

"We have chosen for our daughter the name of MaryAnne's mother–Andrea. What a thing it is to be introduced to one's child. I find a new side to my being that even the gentility of MaryAnne could not produce from my brutal soul."

DAVID PARKIN'S DIARY. JANUARY 18, 1909

❋

"In Philadelphia I had such fortune to discover a most unusual piece, a sixteenth-century brass-and-gold sundial that duplicates the prophet Isaiah's biblical miracle of turning back time.

"'Behold, I will bring again the shadow of the degrees, which is gone down in the sun dial of Ahaz, ten degrees backward. So the sun returned ten degrees, by which degrees it was gone down.' – Isaiah 38:8

"The gilded sundial is lipped to hold water and on one edge a figurine, a Moor, holds taut a line which extends from the center of the dial. The sun's rays, when reflecting from the water, bends the shadow and, for two hours each day, turns back time. Its possessor was unwilling to part with it."

DAVID PARKIN'S DIARY. APRIL 17, 1909

※

"In the year A.D. 69 the Roman emperor Vitellius paid the chief priest of Gaul, whose responsibility it was to determine the beginning and end of spring, a quarter of a billion dollars to extend spring by one minute. The emperor then boasted that he had purchased that which all man cannot. Time.

"Vitellius was a fool."

DAVID PARKIN'S DIARY. APRIL 18, 1909

※

"I find it most peculiar that these old women share their deepest secrets with a man who, but a few months previous, they would have shrunk from in terror had they encountered him on a streetcar."

DAVID PARKIN'S DIARY. AUGUST 1, 1911

※

Author's Note: This is one of my favorite diary entries. I was in the shower when it came to me. As most of my ideas have a thirty second shelf life, I ran out and, still dripping wet, wrote it down on the first paper I could find.

"It would seem that my Andrea is growing so quickly, as if time were advancing at an unnatural pace. At times I wish it were within my power to reach forth my hand and stop the moment–but in this I err. To hold the note is to spoil the song."

DAVID PARKIN'S DIARY. OCTOBER 12, 1911

"It is a question worthy of the philosophers–do we have dreams or do dreams have us? Myself, I do not believe in the mystical or prophetic nature of dreams. But I may be mistaken."

DAVID PARKIN'S DIARY. MARCH 17, 1912

"Is this life, to grasp joy only to fear its escape? The price of happiness is the risk of losing it."

DAVID PARKIN'S DIARY. APRIL 3, 1912

"The most consequential of life's episodes
often begin with the simplest of events."

DAVID PARKIN'S DIARY. OCTOBER 15, 1913

❋

"I know not why I am compelled to write at this time
except as those caught in a torrent seek the surer ground
and those caught in a life's tempests seek the familiar and
the mundane."

DAVID PARKIN'S DIARY. DECEMBER 4, 1913

❋

"How quickly the fabric of our lives unravels. We weave
together protective tapestries of assumption and false belief
that are torn to shreds beneath the malevolent claws of
reality.

"Grief is a merciless schoolmarm."

DAVID PARKIN'S DIARY. DECEMBER 7, 1913

❋

"In Hebrew, 'Mary' means 'bitter.'"

DAVID PARKIN'S DIARY. DECEMBER 8, 1913

※

"There is an oft-misunderstood statement: 'Misery loves company.' To some, it implies that the miserable seek to make others like unto themselves. But it is not the meaning, rather there is a universality in grief, a family of sorrow clinging to each other on the brink of the abyss of despair...

"...I once heard it preached that pain is the currency of salvation. If it is so, surely we have bought heaven."

DAVID PARKIN'S DIARY. DECEMBER 17, 1913

※

"Such darkness besets me. I crave MaryAnne's laughter almost as the drunkard craves his bottle. And for much the same reasons."

DAVID PARKIN'S DIARY. DECEMBER 19, 1913

※

Author's Note: This is a favorite of mine.

"As a child, to visualize nobility was to conjure up images of kings and queens adorned in the majestic, scarlet robes of royalty. As a man, softened by the tutelage of life and time, I have learned a great truth–that true nobility is usually a silent and lonely affair, unaccompanied by the trumpeted fanfare of acclaim. And more times than not, it wears rags."

DAVID PARKIN'S DIARY. DECEMBER 19, 1913

❈

Author's Note: A newspaper reporter once shared with me her own lessons of grief. After years of serving a severely handicapped daughter, her beloved child died. At her daughter's funeral someone thoughtlessly said to her that it must be a relief to finally have it over. The line about the trees came from my daughter, Allyson.

"Today, someone, thinking themselves useful, said to me that it must be a relief to have this 'affair' over with. How indelicately we play each other's heartstrings! How willingly I would carry that pain again for but one glance of her angel face! How she nourished me with her innocence. She once confided in me that the trees are her friends. I asked her how she knew this. She said because they often waved to her. How clearly she saw things! To have such eyes! The trees, for her, shall ever wave to me.

"If I am ever to comfort someone, I will not try to palliate their suffering through foolish reasoning. I will just embrace them and tell them I am heartfelt sorry for their loss."

DAVID PARKIN'S DIARY. DECEMBER 29, 1913

�֍

"What prudery so ritualizes my grief
as to press my letters with black sealing wax."

DAVID PARKIN'S DIARY. DECEMBER 31, 1913

✖

"There are moments, it would seem, that were created in cosmic theater where we are given strange and fantastic tests. In these times, we do not show who we are to God, for surely He must already know, but rather to ourselves."

DAVID PARKIN'S DIARY. DECEMBER 8, 1918

✖

The Letter

The Letter is a story of self-discovery—of picking out the shards of ourselves among the rubble of our broken pasts. The Letter *was written at a personally difficult time. After the initially poor sales of* Timepiece *(which went on to sell nearly a million copies) the naysayers were saying my career as a writer was over. Instead* The Letter *rose up the bestseller lists and became one of the best-selling novels in America that year.*

"MaryAnne will neither enter the parlor nor acknowledge its existence. I cannot fault her for such, as we all have rooms we lock and daren't visit, lest they bring pain."

DAVID PARKIN'S DIARY. FEBRUARY 22, 1932

✳

"Lawrence has never spoken of the hardship of the Depression. Perhaps it is because, for the Negroes, the scenery hasn't much changed."

DAVID PARKIN'S DIARY. SEPTEMBER 10, 1933

✳

"Unlike myself, MaryAnne frequently visits our daughter's grave–oftentimes with weekly regularity. I do not know what she finds in the ritual, nor the particulars of its observance, but at her return her eyes are swollen and her voice spent. It is a reminder of the grief I have unearthed in her life and so deeply buried in mine. I would say that each day the expanse between our hearts widens, except that I cannot be certain. At such great distance it is difficult to perceive the increase of a few extra yards."

DAVID PARKIN'S DIARY. OCTOBER 11, 1933

✳

"At the train station I suddenly had the forceful impression that I would not see MaryAnne again. The premonitions that we so quickly dismiss are sometimes our truest glances of reality."

DAVID PARKIN'S DIARY. OCTOBER 11, 1933

✳

"From our first babblings to our last word,
we make but one statement, and that is our life."

DAVID PARKIN'S DIARY. OCTOBER 11, 1933

✳

Author's Note: I am especially fond of the last two lines of this entry.

"I feel so lost. No. To be lost is to not know where one is–and I am all too sure. I am alone. My heart, my love, has been torn from me and I am consumed by the pain of that loss. Yet I feel MaryAnne around me as keenly as before. Maybe more so. For I see her absence in all the evidences of the home that she left behind.

"I am a fool. What selfishness so blinded my heart that I could not see that she still required its nourishment?

"My pen rambles with more foolishness. I mourn what I am missing and the pain that pierces my heart–not hers. This is the paradox that keeps MaryAnne from my reach–for to go after her, for my heart's sake, is to be unworthy of her. Could it be that to truly love a thing is not to desire it, but to desire happiness for it? If so, I cannot have her back, to relieve my heart at the expense of hers. If I truly love her.

"And I do love her. More than my own life I love her. I can only hope that she might return. Yet hope is oftentimes the cruelest of virtues.

"How did I come to such a dark place? I don't know where my road now leads but I fear the shadowlands that lie ahead. But it is not the darkness of the path I fear. Just the loneliness of the trail."

DAVID PARKIN'S DIARY. OCTOBER 21, 1933

"Even as I withheld my love from MaryAnne, she had never stopped filling me with hers. I had never supposed how cold my world would be without her warmth."

DAVID PARKIN'S DIARY. NOVEMBER 2, 1933

❋

"Catherine delivered to me a letter today that she supposed was written by my mother. I am uncertain whether it should be celebrated or incinerated."

DAVID PARKIN'S DIARY. NOVEMBER 9, 1933

❋

"Despite plans to the contrary, I ended up meeting Victoria's niece. She was not at all like Victoria–that is to say, she was pleasant."

DAVID PARKIN'S DIARY. DECEMBER 15, 1933

❋

"A broken heart is always looking for a mend."

DAVID PARKIN'S DIARY. DECEMBER 15, 1933

❋

"I stopped by Lawrence's this evening and, in the course of our visit, he hinted at something I had never before imagined–that he had once been married. It is a peculiar thing to believe that you know someone intimately only to find that you really do not. It is like finishing a book only to discover that you have missed several key chapters."

DAVID PARKIN'S DIARY. DECEMBER 17, 1933

✳

"There is nothing so healing to oneself
as to heal another."

DAVID PARKIN'S DIARY. DECEMBER 26, 1933

✳

"It is a peculiar domain the mind enters when one is asleep. Why it chooses one landscape over another, or horror over joy, is the most baffling of mysteries. My nightmares have returned."

DAVID PARKIN'S DIARY. DECEMBER 27, 1933

✳

"I do not remember much of my mother,
but that she left me. And that, perhaps, is too much."

DAVID PARKIN'S DIARY. DECEMBER 28, 1933

✹

"Chicago boasts a profusion of theaters and cabarets—
myriads more than I had presumed. One often does not
realize the bulk of the haystack or the meagerness of the
needle until one has sorted the first bale."

DAVID PARKIN'S DIARY. JANUARY 6, 1934

✹

"Still no word from MaryAnne. My feelings cannot be
far distant from those of the dustbowl farmer who, looking
out over his withered fields to the blanched sky above, won-
ders why it will not rain."

DAVID PARKIN'S DIARY. JANUARY 11, 1934

✹

"Dierdre is a woman endowed with the rare quality of contentment—the ability to find the joy possessed in each circumstance as mysteriously as the desert aborigine finds water in the parched desert…"

DAVID PARKIN'S DIARY. JANUARY 11, 1934

"It is strange to me that two women could share such close proximity in my mind, yet be worlds apart. And only one of them cares to be there.

DAVID PARKIN'S DIARY. JANUARY 12, 1934

"It is folly of our species that we reserve the greatest bouquets for our dead."

DAVID PARKIN'S DIARY. JANUARY 12, 1934

"It is of little consolation to learn of my mother's wretched past. For as miserable as it was she still chose it over me."

DAVID PARKIN'S DIARY. JANUARY 12, 1934

"There is no more constant companion
than the specter of regret."

DAVID PARKIN'S DIARY. JANUARY 12, 1934

Author's Note: I am rather fond of this one.

"It has been a mistake living my life in the past.
One cannot ride a horse backwards and still hold its reins."

DAVID PARKIN'S DIARY. JANUARY 13, 1934

*Author's Note: I wrote this after my grandfather suffered
a debilitating stroke.*

"It is an awkward thing for a loved one to retain their
breath but lose their faculties. I feel as though my heart has
been cheated, as I have lost a friend and am not allowed to
grieve his passing."

DAVID PARKIN'S DIARY. JANUARY 16, 1934

"I came home to find that MaryAnne had returned. She promptly made it clear that she does not intend to stay. My heart, of necessity, has become acrobatic."

DAVID PARKIN'S DIARY. JANUARY 16, 1934

✹

"When we bury someone we love, we must also bury a part of our heart. But we should not bemoan this loss. Our hearts, perhaps, are all they can take with them."

DAVID PARKIN'S DIARY. JANUARY 28, 1934

✹

"The sexton is a peculiar man, enslaved by the dominion of ritual and constancy. His vocation is well chosen as nothing is so reliable as death."

DAVID PARKIN'S DIARY. JANUARY 29, 1934

✹

"I have heard it preached that on Judgment Day our sins will be shouted from the rooftops. I have come to believe that if this is so, it will not be by some heavenly tribunal or something loathsome that crawls beneath, but from our own countenance screaming out to the world who we really are–when the kind and the good, no matter how plain in this life, will shine forth like suns, while the loathsome and dark will cower from their light."

"If Heaven is a place where there are no secrets, it would, for some, also be Hell."

DAVID PARKIN'S DIARY. JANUARY 29, 1934

※

"There is no confection so sweet as joyful reunion."

DAVID PARKIN'S DIARY. FEBRUARY 2, 1934

※

"The noble causes of life have always seemed foolish to the uninspired. But this is of small concern. I worry less about the crucified than those who pounded the nails."

DAVID PARKIN'S DIARY. MARCH 4, 1934

※

My beloved David,

No matter how I write, the words fall so cruel, I wish I could use them more sparingly. This is farewell, my love. I shall not return from London. I do not know anymore if my departure is right or wrong, I have reasoned until I can think no more—all I know is what I feel and what I can bear. Or cannot. I can no longer endure the pain of your alienation. Your love was my sun, David, and the walls you have built around your heart have deprived me of its warmth until my heart has wilted. My departure is only the final act of a separation that took place years ago and what we have prolonged has only mocked the beauty of what we once shared. It is with heartbreak that I admit that our marriage died with our daughter.

I know that you love me—as I do you. This is what has given wings to my flight, for love is a traitorous emotion. Never once did you hold it against me that you were not Andrea's birth father, yet it is thrown back at you daily as you cannot give me more children and you blame yourself for losing our only. You did not lose our daughter, David. Andrea's death was caused by the cruel actions of evil men. You were nothing but courageous and compassionate. Shall we not stand up to evil because it threatens our personal situation? If we do not, evil will always prevail. You taught me this and although you may know that you did the right thing, you do not believe it. There is a difference, and in that difference I have lost my husband. I cannot change your heart, I can only break the cycle of our pain.

Forgive me for my weakness–for bidding farewell in ink, not words. I could not face you. I was afraid that you would implore me to stay and I would not be able to resist. How could I deny the man I cherish more than all? I once gave you my life, David, but I had never imagined that I would steal away yours. I give it back to you. I beg you to not pursue me. Go and be free.

You are forever in my heart.

Mary

My dearest Sophia,

I do not hope that you will ever read this letter. For if you do, your mama and papa have failed in our duty to protect you from my identity. But as you have learned of me, there are things you must now know. You should know how much I love you. A child should know their father's love. You may ask why I was not in your life–why it was so important to us to hide myself from you. It is because we loved you that I gave you up–that people would not hurt you. You know, by now, that your papa is a Negro. Your mama and I didn't want you to know that you had mixed blood. We wanted you to have a life my skin color could not offer. The world has taken you away from me, but they cannot take you from my heart. I did see you once. I came and stood alongside the road where you walked from school. Even though I had come across half the country, when I saw you near I felt afraid of how you might treat a strange Negro and I wanted to turn back. You stopped and asked me kindly if I was a stranger in town and needed some help to find my way. Do you recall? I thanked you and said I knew just where I needed to go. Back home. My heart was so proud I thought it would burst.

I never got the chance to say it to your face, but I love you my darling.

Your Papa

※

March 17, 1912

To the proprietors of the Gaiety.
Messrs.

With the closure of the Gaiety, you have effectively ended my career, as my life, for they are the same. Tonight, I shall throw myself from the Troop Street bridge. May my demise haunt your despicable lives and the curtain fall on all of your ambitions, as they have mine. I regret having been enslaved by the bonds of my ambitions. But I confess a greater regret, that I mistook this pantomime for something real–a life that might have brought lasting joy instead of the vaporous illusion of fame and fortune. My husband died in my absence. I have not seen my son since he was but six. I once fantasized that one day he would come to the theater to see me perform, and that our reunion would be grand. I am now certain that he should only know the bitterness of betrayal.

Adieu.

Rosalyn King

The Locket

Having bid farewell to the Parkins of The Christmas Box *trilogy,* The Locket *marked the beginning of a new series—new lives and new lessons to learn.* The Locket *is a story of second chances. It contains my favorite diary entries.*

Author's Note: I have received a great many requests for reprints of this entry.

"Believe. Believe in your destiny and the star from which it shines. Believe you have been sent from God as an arrow pulled from his own bow.

"It is the single universal trait which the great of this earth have all shared, while the shadows are fraught with ghosts who roam the winds with mournful wails of regret on their lips.

"Believe as if your life depended upon it, for indeed it does."

ESTHER HUISH'S DIARY

⚜

"As I lie in bed listening to the toil of my body beneath the infirmities of age, my heart wanders again to Betheltown and I wonder how it is that, through the same sorcery of time that has brought me to my end, Betheltown has become less heartbreak than joy. And less memory than dream."

ESTHER HUISH'S DIARY

❧

"The Arcadia is unlike that chill, tile institution that I was brought here from. The small difference between it and a sepulcher was movie night."

ESTHER HUISH'S DIARY

❧

"... Not all heroes are painted on white stallions."

ESTHER HUISH'S DIARY

❧

"Today a man was shot in Betheltown. While murder is commonplace in Goldstrike, this is the first of such incidents in Betheltown. The dispute was over an abandoned claim of the Layola mine...Money is a cheap way to sell one's soul."

"Betheltown is dying. Only the Salisbury mine remains, but it too will soon close. Only a few of us remain to die with the town. I suppose that I should not wonder at my present circumstance.

"That which we expect of life is indeed all that it ever can be."

"There are those who, in the same breath, pray for the poor and for the blessing of never encountering them."

Author's Note: I acknowledge the influence of C.S. Lewis's Screwtape Letters *in this entry.*

"Today a group of miners organized to bar negroes from working in the mines. The greatest evils of this world have always been performed by committee."

ESTHER HUISH'S DIARY

❊

"An old acquaintance of my father's came through Betheltown today. He was on his way back from California where he has amassed a small fortune. He boasted greatly at my father's expense. There are those who go about their lives sharpening their egos on the grindstone of other's failures."

ESTHER HUISH'S DIARY

❊

"How often the course of a life is changed in one pulse of a heart."

ESTHER HUISH'S DIARY

❊

"Today, a Mr. Foster booked a room in the inn. He is a wealthy man and had come to Betheltown at the prospect of purchasing the Pate Mine. He spoke condescendingly to me as I served him his dinner. Then I suppose he decided me attractive as he expressed his desire for me to dine with him. I declined his offer. Rich company, like rich food, is often a cause of indigestion."

"The most difficult of decisions are often not the ones in which we cannot determine the correct course, rather the ones in which we are certain of the path but fear the journey."

"I have wondered if I am trying to force a life. While the life I lead may not match the picture in my head, perhaps the one offered me is just as full of joy, its pigments just as bright, just not what I expected."

"It was a festive Christmas Eve in Betheltown, and we gathered at the church to sing and worship and feast. I returned near midnight and shortly afterward a couple came to the inn seeking lodging. We had no vacancy and as I was about to turn them out, the great irony of the circumstance was manifest. I gave them my room for the night and slept in the kitchen."

ESTHER HUISH'S DIARY

※

"There comes to each life at least one Betheltown. But it comes only once and we dare not ask for more."

ESTHER HUISH'S DIARY

※

"It is folly, I suspect, to commence each morning with a letter to my lost love and conclude it with my diary, thereby bleeding at both ends of the day."

ESTHER HUISH'S DIARY

※

"A handsome young man came this evening to inquire for lodging, his intent being to stay in Betheltown for some while. I must remind myself that sunsets too are beautiful, before they leave you cold, dark, and alone."

ESTHER HUISH'S DIARY

✦

"There are those who clutch to resentment like it were a treasure of great worth. This is foolishness. The question to be asked is not how badly we were wronged, but what are we profited by our unforgiveness?"

ESTHER HUISH'S DIARY

✦

"There have been too many departures in my life. I have yet to find the good in goodbye or the well in farewell."

ESTHER HUISH'S DIARY

✦

"At the arrival of this new year I can only wonder if Thomas will return, though I fear the answer. There are those who will read the last page of a book first. But it is not me. I believe that it is fortunate that we are allowed to turn just one page of our lives at a time."

ESTHER HUISH'S DIARY

"That which we spend our lives hoping for is often no more than another chance to do what we should have done to begin with."

ESTHER HUISH'S DIARY

"Winter is difficult in Betheltown. But I believe it is God's plan that we suffer the cold of Winter that we might know the warmth of Spring."

ESTHER HUISH'S DIARY

"The winds of oppression that extinguish the flame of freedom in some only fan the fire of resistance in others."

ESTHER HUISH'S DIARY

"...even the most horrible of nightmares
is laced with the promise of dawn."

❧

"There are more lines today in the looking glass.
Time is the warden of all flesh."

❧

"Tonight I took a stroll under the stars with Thomas. He
spoke profoundly of trivial things which, I suppose, is better than the inverse. Under the moon's glow he somehow
looked different to me. Perhaps it is, has always been, that
the moon gives visage only to that which is already within us."

❧

"It is my observation that too often this world
builds monuments to those it stoned in the flesh."

❧

"When I consider the hardships that some others must face, my troubles seem foolish and petty—a succession of quixotic battles. To God, perhaps, they are all windmills."

Author's Note: How often I have considered this.

"There are times that I have been tempted to protect my heart from further disappointment with cynicism...But it would be like poisoning oneself to avoid being murdered."

Author's Note: This is one of my favorites.

"There are those whose primary ambition in life is to leave their names chiseled on some small corner of this globe. But this is folly. The greatest tragedy is not to die unknown by strangers, but unloved by our companions."

"Oftentimes the difference between a lynch mob
and a square dance is a good fiddler."

ESTHER HUISH'S DIARY

❧

"A man came to the inn today seeking a room. There was
a coldness to his mien which left me chill. I bore false wit-
ness in telling him that there were no vacancies. There is a
reason that there are people whom we instinctively distrust.
That which we endeavor to conceal from the world is
revealed in our countenances."

ESTHER HUISH'S DIARY

❧

My dearest Michael,

I would so rather say these things to your face, but as we both know, life doesn't often take requests. So I've asked Helen to help me with this letter. Just in case. I suppose this is a will of sorts. First, I do not know yet the outcome of the trial. I cannot know if you are reading this in a cage. I can only hope my letter and the signatures of your friends were of some benefit. I have faith that you will be free, so I shall write this letter as such and not take counsel from my fears.

I would like you to have my letters and my diaries. They are the scars of my heart's wound. A heart you helped to heal. They hold my deepest feelings and that is what, most of all, I would like to leave with you. I also bequeath to you my furniture and my Bible. The furniture is hand carved and antique. The bureau was crafted by Marius Morrell, who gained some notoriety as a joiner, so there may be some value to it. It is sturdy at any rate. The Bible belonged to my father. It is old but its value is in its words, not material.

In the bottom drawer of my bureau, buried beneath my letters, is a leather portfolio. For years, William and I put every extra penny we earned into war bonds which were meant to be used for Matthew's care after we were both gone. I have not had much need for money and the bonds have long since matured. There should be enough to pay for your schooling and some of your expenses.

In the top drawer of the bureau is a velvet pouch containing two heirlooms. The first is my locket. I would like you to return it to Betheltown for me–to lay it by the hearth of the fireplace where I left my love so many years ago. I had once thought to be buried in Betheltown, but I no longer hold that desire. The locket will be sufficient. I have helped Helen to draw a map. I am certain that the roads will be grown over, but you will know the place.

In the pouch is also the engagement ring of Thomas's that I retrieved from the fireplace's hearth. What you do with it is for you to decide. I have not been one to share advice (coming from me, what could it be worth?) but this much I know. You are good. And there is more to that than is contained in all the world's treasure houses. To come from the fringes of humanity and remain clean of cynicism is as high an ambition as a soul may aspire to. Do not be afraid to choose good for yourself, Michael. I know you have never considered this, it is not your way, but Faye would be truly fortunate to have you.

I am proud of you, Michael. As proud, I suspect, as your own mother might be. If I am to see her in some other realm I shall offer her my gratitude for lending me her son for a while. I do not know what more I could say than what I wrote in my letter to the jury–if my son were whole, I would have hoped that he would someday be like you.

God does allow us second chances. But sometimes they're just best given to someone else.

Go well, my dear friend,

Esther

The Looking Glass

The Looking Glass, *ultimately, is a love story about the divine nature of mankind. It is about seeing ourselves for who we really are.*

"It has been nearly three months since I arrived in Goldstrike. It is a barbarous camp as thirsty for blood as it is for the noble metals. This last week I witnessed a man gunned down in a barbershop and the proprietor did not so much as interrupt the lathering of his client.

"I have become proficient at cards and can turn an ace as well as I once turned holy writ. Cards are more profitable than prospecting and more predictable than God. There is more gold to be had from fools than in the entire range of mountains and it is considerably easier drawing it forth."

HUNTER BELL'S DIARY. MAY 29, 1857

"I have fled yet another town. It is a precarious line I walk; one step ahead of the noose and one step behind peace."

HUNTER BELL'S DIARY. JUNE 2, 1857

"Though I continue to rebuff her advances, the boarding house owner's daughter is well-dispositioned toward me. At times, hearts are the most traitorous of devices. They tumble headlong and blindly toward obvious dangers while they obstinately protect us from that which would likely do us the most good."

HUNTER BELL'S DIARY. MAY 28, 1857

"The dreams still haunt me, leaving me in the dawn wet with tears. It is true, there are moments in one's life more memorable than entire years. But these moments are those usually wished forgotten."

HUNTER BELL'S DIARY. JUNE 3, 1857

"I have ridden two days by horse from Goldstrike into the solitude of Utah's desert. I find it peculiar that I am less lonely in the isolation of the desert than the bustle of Goldstrike. Loneliness is often heightened by company."

HUNTER BELL'S DIARY. JUNE 3, 1857

"I have discovered gold as thick as sin in a creekbed in Goldstrike. I do not count it yet as either a blessing or a curse. Time will tell. Gold is an able servant but a cruel master."

HUNTER BELL'S DIARY. JUNE 6, 1857

"I made the day-and-a-half ride from Goldstrike to the Great Salt Lake City, then made a spectacle of myself by loading down a wagon with enough supplies to keep until the Second Coming. I was noticed by all and no doubt I will be joined by a few prospectors after my return to Bethel. As sure as success will destroy a man, it will just as assuredly be imitated."

HUNTER BELL'S DIARY. JUNE 9, 1857

"The miners have crashed upon my town like a wave from the great ocean of humanity. How quickly it is forgotten that Midas's gift was a curse, not a blessing."

HUNTER BELL'S DIARY. JUNE 29, 1857

"I do not wonder at the cruelty of this world, as it seems the nature of it. I find myself more perplexed at why there is good at all."

HUNTER BELL'S DIARY. AUGUST 19, 1857

"Is man good and bent evil by society, or is he born evil, and kept straight by society's heavy hand? Most disturbing to me about this question is not its answer, but the reason for which it is most often invoked."

HUNTER BELL'S DIARY. AUGUST 19, 1857

"It is silent now, the blizzard has paused and left the moment still. I think about them both at such times–roaming the shadowlands of memory amidst the shards of my broken heart. I fear less the hell that must assuredly await me in the beyond than that which is born of my own life and its remembrances. I have considered that they are, perhaps, the same–that Hell is nothing more than a clear recognition of what we are and what we might have been..."

HUNTER BELL'S DIARY. DECEMBER 8, 1857

"By some conspiracy of Heaven or Hell (I know not which), a woman has been placed in my keeping. I am reminded of the proverb: A strange woman is a narrow pit."

HUNTER BELL'S DIARY. DECEMBER 9, 1857

"There are those who deny the existence of God and there are those who have witnessed too much to deny the unseen world, and deny themselves of the love of God. In this I am the most hopeless of men. For there is not much hope to be found in hating a God, if you believe in Him. And there is not much future in it."

HUNTER BELL'S DIARY. DECEMBER 10, 1857

Author's Note: I have pinned this quote to my office wall. It is true that the greatest strides I have made in my life were because of my failures.

"I have learned a great truth of life. We do not succeed in spite of our challenges and difficulties, but rather, pre-cisely because of them."

HUNTER BELL'S DIARY. DECEMBER 13, 1857

"The woman, Pandora, has read what my love once wrote."

HUNTER BELL'S DIARY. DECEMBER 26, 1857

"I have learned much about loss from their pain. Oftentimes it takes the darkness of another's grief to shed light on our own."

HUNTER BELL'S DIARY. DECEMBER 28, 1857

"The truth of our selves is too often blurred by the capricious image of our self-perception. I believe it is among man's greatest quests of life, not just to see life as it really is, but to see his part in it."

HUNTER BELL'S DIARY. DECEMBER 28, 1857

"The greatest shackles we bear in this life
are those forged by our own fears."

HUNTER BELL'S DIARY. JANUARY 7, 1858

"I have made a grave mistake. I have carelessly handled a heart entrusted to mine. And in so doing I have broken both."

HUNTER BELL'S DIARY. JANUARY 7, 1858

"Again, I am encompassed by walls of solitude. I believe that Hell must be a confinement of our own contrivance, laid brick by brick, until, by our own cowardice and compromise, we have isolated ourselves from all love. And from all that is lovely."

HUNTER BELL'S DIARY. JANUARY 8, 1858

"Nowhere is royalty less to be trusted
than in a deck of cards."

HUNTER BELL'S DIARY. JANUARY 10, 1858

"Sometimes it seems what we should
desire most is not to desire."

HUNTER BELL'S DIARY. JANUARY 10, 1858

"It is a peculiar justice they practice in the West; a mockery of the law overseen by the dishonorable Judge Lynch with his 10,000 arms and two bum eyes."

HUNTER BELL'S DIARY. SACRAMENTO, 1856

"I consider with wonderment the path which has led me to this place of tranquility.

Though one does not forget the wounds of the past, scars can bring gratitude if we will consider the healer. There is not a day that I do not think of him. Though I have peace in my heart, it only makes my longing for him more clear.

My Hunter has given me more reason to hope for an afterlife than every scripture penned and every prayer offered."

QUAYE BELL'S DIARY. APRIL 16, 1901

My dearest Hunter,

If only my lips could use such words as my heart so casually speaks—that the clouds of my mind might not obscure the sun of my love. But I, of all women, should be most content with my lot and express in love's duty what my words strain to share.

You are my light and one true dream. You are my faith and my religion and I lay my heart at the altar of your love. How glad such submission!

Oh, dear husband, see how quietly my pen endeavors to speak what my soul wishes to shout. Thus I gift to you this book and borrow another's words and if my pen cannot claim ownership, my heart fears not to plagiarize...

"The face of all the world is changed, I think, since first I heard the footsteps of thy soul..."

With all my tender affections,
Rachel

Life's Lessons

ON LIFE

. . . life's greatest philosophy is not handed down in stoic texts and dusty tomes, but lived, in each breath and act of human compassion. For love has always demanded sacrifice, and no greater love is there than that for which our lives are traded.

And in this great cause of spiritual evolution we are all called to be martyrs, to die each of us in the quest of a higher realm and loftier ideals, that we may know God.

And what if there is nothing else? What if all life ends in the silent void of death? Then is it all in vain? I think not. For love, for the sake of love, will always be enough. And if our lives are but a single flash in the dark hollow of eternity, then, if, but for the briefest of moments, we shine–then how brilliantly our light has burned. And as the starlight knows no boundary of space or time, so, too, our illumination will shine forth throughout all eternity, for darkness has no power to quell such light. And this is a lesson we must all learn and take to heart–that all light is eternal and all love is light. And it must forever be so.

THE LETTER

ॐ

"You once asked me why I collected clocks."

MaryAnne nodded.

"I have given this question a great deal of thought since then. A clock is a strange invention. A collection of cogs and gears that are always in motion, yet accomplish nothing. Not like a pump that provides water or a cotton gin that leaves something useful. A clock just moves without thought or meaning–worthless without interpretation." His eyes focused on the clock in condemnation. "It is just motion." He turned and looked into his new wife's eyes. "And so has been my life. I have moved, not with feeling, but because it is all that I could see to do. You have given my motion meaning."

MaryAnne looked into David's face. "I have given you my life, David."

"And in so doing, you have given me mine."

TIMEPIECE

ᏮᎿ

Poetry, like life, is its own justification.

TIMEPIECE

ᏮᎿ

"I just want to say thank you for this opportunity.
I don't believe life owes us anything but that."

THE LOCKET

ᏮᎿ

"I learned what I needed to learn—that it doesn't really matter what happened back then. There is nothing anyone can do with the past, except let it fade." He swallowed. "As I stood looking out over the bridge my mother jumped from, I had this remarkable moment of clarity. Do you know what I realized?"

MaryAnne began to tremble and did not turn, for she did not want David to see her tears.

"I realized how much I missed you. And that all that really matters in my life is earning your trust and getting you back. And then I thought, I will never get that chance, because you will never return. I understood the hopelessness my mother felt. Because when you lose something that precious, you have really lost. And I, too, wanted to jump."

MaryAnne began to sob quietly.

"And then I had the strangest thought. What if I jumped? And then in some other realm I encountered Andrea and she asked me what I had done with my life since she left. And I had to tell her that I had thrown away everything that I loved. That was my great epiphany, when I realized that what I had been doing was really no different than what my mother had done. That I had also abandoned myself and those that depended on me. I didn't get on a train to do it, but it was just as real." David cleared his throat. "I haven't been the same since. I don't know how to tell you this, because it just sounds like I am trying to get you to stay." His voice cracked. "And more than anything I want you to stay..." He dropped his head. "No, that's wrong. More than anything I want you to want to stay."

THE LETTER

🕉

She stopped me at the doorway. "Michael."

"Yes?"

"Do you suppose life gives us second chances?"

"What do you mean?"

"If we've made a mistake in our lives, do you think that God or fate gives us a second chance to make it right?"

I considered the question. "I don't know. But we'd probably just make the same mistake over again."

Her countenance fell and her sadness resonated through her voice. "Thank you for reading to me."

I was unhappy to have contributed to her sadness. "Maybe I'm wrong. I just don't think I've seen any second chances in my life."

"Perhaps you don't know how to recognize them."

THE LOCKET

🕉

In that moment the loathing he felt for the vigilantes was matched by that which he felt for himself.

He glanced down the darkened street toward the lit saloon, then back at the boardinghouse.

He could run. He knew how to run. Just as he could have left Quaye to the wolves, he could leave her to the animal with whom she now lived and hope that with enough time and liquor his memory of her would die.

Or he could choose life. At that pivotal moment, it occurred to him that with all his schooling in theology he had, perhaps, missed the entire point of his studies, the very crux of the gospel he had professed to believe. That the measure of a person's heart, the barometer of good or evil, was nothing more than the extent of their willingness to choose life over death. That the path of God was, simply, the path of life, abundant and eternal. And this is where he failed, for to choose life is to choose sorrow as well as joy, pain as well as pleasure. When Hunter had buried Rachel, he buried along with her his heart, lest it might heal and feel and grow again. And in so doing he had chosen more than death, he had chosen damnation itself, for damnation is nothing more than to stop a thing in its eternal progression. In that first flight from West Chester he had run not only from the horror and pain of death but from life itself.

THE LOOKING GLASS

ତ୍ତ

ON LOVE

I am not a believer in love at first sight. For love, in its truest form, is not the thing of starry-eyed or star-crossed lovers, it is far more organic, requiring nurturing and time to fully bloom, and, as such, seen best not in its callow youth but in its wrinkled maturity.

Like all living things, love, too, struggles against hardship, and in the process sheds its fatuous skin to expose one composed of more than just a storm of emotion–one of loyalty and divine friendship. Agape. And though it may be temporarily blinded by adversity, it never gives in or up, holding tight to lofty ideals that transcend this earth and time–while its counterfeit simply concludes it was mistaken and quickly runs off to find the next real thing.

THE LETTER

৩৫

"I love you, not for the things you have, or even what you might have or might become someday–but because of who you are right now and how you make me feel. I love the goodness of your heart. I have friends who have married rich boys with poor hearts and I pity them, in their new cars and big new homes for all their poverty."

THE LOCKET

৩৫

"We all got things under our skin. Everybody does. Like a glass sliver. Can't see nothin' there, but it works its way in deeper until it gets to festerin' and hurts so that we're ready to just cut the whole thing out"

David poured himself another glass.

"Comes a time that everyone needs to find their answers. Need to connect with their past. You ain't crazy, David, you just filled with the spirit of Elijah."

"What is that?"

"Like the Bible talk 'bout. Turnin' of the children's hearts to the parents."

David looked down and frowned. "Then I get to thinking that I should let it go—maybe there is nothing to be gained. Maybe my mother was like MaryAnne—she fell out of love."

Lawrence groaned incredulously. "MaryAnne never stopped lovin' you. Lord, David, you talk 'bout love like it a hole. Somethin' you can fall in and out of."

"Isn't it?"

His aged face wrinkled in indignation. "That ain't love at all, just squirrel fever. Just a storm of emotions." Lawrence grimaced. "Man sees a pretty skirt and calls it love. Most women folk ain't much smarter. Give more credence to butterflies than friendship. Real love's ain't that way. It's more like a tree or plant or somethin'."

"How's that?"

"Grows if you take mind to it. But it takes work and sacrifices. No one stand back of a neglected tree and watch it

71

die and say, "Guess that tree just ain't suppose to live.'
Only a fool would talk like that. But people do it all the
time with their loves."

THE LETTER

৪৩

It is, perhaps, the greatest irony of love. That which we
truly love, we must be willing to give up for its own benefit. And in this I knew how much Faye meant to me. For
as breathless as the possibility of losing her left me, there
was no question in my mind that I would lay down my
heart as a stepping-stone for her to reach her dreams. To
do less would be a counterfeit of love, a forgery with no
value other than what self-indulgent fraud could be had of
it. That's what I knew. At least, that's what I thought I
knew. What I had not factored into the equation, perhaps
never dared to, is that I was the greater part of her dreams.

THE LOCKET

৪৩

"I believe it a great irony that I learned of life
from one dying, and of love from one so lonely."

THE LOCKET

৪৩

"It took me years to understand that when you truly care about someone, you must focus on more than your own desires. To truly love something is not to desire a thing, but to desire its happiness. That's why love requires sacrifices. Sometimes painful ones." He paused for emphasis. "Some of the other boys Faye brings home I could never have this conversation with, but you're different. You understand my meaning."

His casual injection of "other boys" stung me, but I did not show it. "I think that I do."

"I don't need to tell you that life is hard. You never know what's around the next bend, and sometimes it knocks the wind out of you. That's the way marriage is as well. How often do you see a couple years down the line still staring goo-goo eyed at each other? It just doesn't happen." He leaned forward, his brow bent in grave inquiry. "Do you know why?"

"No, sir."

"It is because romantic love is an illusion. It portends an eternal round of ecstatic bliss with love conquering all. That's how all relationships start. But then the silver lining begins to tarnish and the honeymoon ends. Pretty soon she's complaining because you haven't been out to dinner for a month and there's not enough in the bank account, even while your boss is breaking your back." He took another drink. "All relationships start on fire. But the embers cool."

"Is that how it is with you and Mrs. Murrow?"

He didn't like my question, and for the first time I detected the anger that simmered beneath his calm facade. Then, inexplicably, his lips rose in a whimsical smile as if we had been playfully sparring and I had just scored a point.

"You do understand that romance will disappear. And then what have you? Only the life that you have built for yourselves."

I shifted uncomfortably in my chair. "It may sound naive, but I think you are wrong. I believe it's after the honeymoon ends that true love begins. It's in the hard times that the greater virtues of love reveal themselves, like tolerance and patience and kindness."

THE LOCKET

෨෬

David took her hand in his. It was the first time that he had touched her in this way and it filled him with a strange electricity.

"In the wedding vow, they say for better or worse. In sickness and in health. For richer or poorer. It would seem that the only thing certain about the alliance is a lot of uncertainty."

MaryAnne looked into his eyes. His gaze was direct and kind.

"I am not afraid of uncertainty or responsibility–it is what life is made of. But I am afraid that I will not meet another woman like you. And that you will not have me."

TIMEPIECE

ରେ

To harrowed darkness came such light,
From lofty realms of hope descends,
To where the quiet, broken lay,
Despairing, sullen realm of night.
Amidst the dark, a brilliant sun,
She lifts the shards of shattered dreams,
and pressed the sharp against her heart,
With her sweet blood she made them one.

THE LOCKET

ରେ

"Marrying you would be like winning the lottery—one of those good things that happen to other people. I've always assumed it was just somewhere off the horizon. It seems that's where good things always lie."

Faye smiled sweetly. "I know we're young, Michael, but I think I'm ready. My parents would have me wait until everything in my life is neat and tidy with hospital corners. But life isn't best lived that way. I see couples who have built their lives together, struggling through the hard times. Some say it's the best years of their lives. I want that. I don't want some by-the-book life with neatly penned entrances like it were a Broadway production. I want to live it. For better or worse." She kissed me on the cheek. "I love you, Michael. You're what I've always wanted."

THE LOCKET

&G

ON CREATIVITY

"...creative causes must be dictated by passion,
and without passion we are doomed to mediocrity."

THE LOCKET

ೂಂ

ON ACTION

Gibbs sighed, then reluctantly stood. "We have been through a lot together and you always seem to come out on top. But I have a bad feeling about this. I grant you that what you are doing is noble in its own way, but the cost of what you are doing is too great."

David shook his head. "No, Gibbs. Only the cost of doing nothing is ever too great."

TIMEPIECE

ೂಂ

"I met him last spring," MaryAnne answered. "I have not known him for very long."

Victoria's face contorted in pretense to some awful knowledge. "Well, I would be ill used to not warn you of David. He is a controversial sort."

"Controversial?"

"It is quite well known." She set her plate on the linen cloth of a buffet, then leaned close to MaryAnne. "He associates quite openly with the Negroes and makes absolutely no attempt to hide it. It is as if he is not ashamed of it."

MaryAnne felt her cheeks flush with indignation. Victoria continued.

"You should be apprised. Of course, I should be pleased if this was the worst of his vices. There is much more that you should know." She paused to fan herself. "But this is not the time or place. It is disloyal of me to eat his cake and poison his name."

"Yes," MaryAnne replied, "perhaps you should just poison his cake and be done with it."

TIMEPIECE

෬෬

ON ADVERSITY

Author's Note: One night I was driving home from a speaking engagement when my daughter Jenna looked out into the night and said, "Dad, look how pretty the stars are." It was then that the last line of this passage came to me.

It is often during the worst of times that we see the best of humanity–awakening within the most ordinary of us that which is most sublime. I do not believe that it is circumstance that produces such greatness any more than it is the canvas that makes the artist. Adversity merely presents the surface on which we render our souls' most exacting likeness. It is in the darkest skies that stars are best seen.

THE LETTER

ജ

ON AGING

I will never cease to be amazed by our species' keen ability for denial. Prior to my coming to the Arcadia, I had never given much thought to growing old or to those who had. It was not a conscious evasion, simply the consequence of circumstance. I didn't know anyone elderly. Both of my parents had died by the age of forty-five. I had no close grandparents, on my father's side by choice and on my mother's side by death, so the elderly remained to me people of a foreign culture, as removed from my everyday thoughts as the French—a culture I had occasional contact with, knew a few words of their native tongue, but had little relevance to my daily life. While this may be understandable, the difference to me is that we will not all be Parisians someday—but unless death plays its trump card in an early hand, we will all grow old. But like I said, we are keen at denial, and old age, like death, is always someone else's destination.

THE LOCKET

&ᴑ

"Do you suppose that in biblical times they named leper colonies?"

"I've never considered that. I suppose so. Why?"

"They give these homes names that make them sound like paradises. Arcadia. Elysian Hills, Green Pastures, Golden Living. They should name them after Western towns, like Last Stop or Death Valley. Places we go to die."

I gripped her hand, closing my eyes tightly. She continued speaking, her voice hoarse with grief. "There's no difference between this place and a leper colony. We gather all those with like affliction so they can die out of sight. Only, age is more frightening than leprosy. It's an affliction all must face." Her voice turned gruff. "Do not pity me. Pity yourself. The young are too afraid. They hold on so tightly to their lives that they squeeze the joy out of them." She closed her eyes and she was quiet, and I could hear her swallow. "Pity is a pathetic thing."

THE LOCKET

೦೦

ON GRIEF AND SORROW

"Are you warm enough, MaryAnne?"

MaryAnne diverted her gaze and nodded. Catherine looked ahead into the unending horizon of white, sniffed, then rubbed her nose. "I have tried to reason what to say that might be of comfort," she said, her voice weak from emotion. "It is too lofty an ambition for words." She fell silent again.

A solitary magpie lit on an ice-caked sundial, cried out into the gray winter air, then flew back into its cold grasp.

MaryAnne's eyes stared vacantly ahead.

"I have done the same," she said softly. "I tell myself that she will live in my memory. There should be comfort in this." She wiped her reddened eyes with her sleeve. "I should not say 'live.' 'Embalmed' is a better word. Each memory embalmed and dressed in grave clothes with a headstone marking the time and place as a reminder that I will never see my Andrea again."

Catherine said nothing, but looked somberly on, her eyes moistened with her friend's pain.

"There are things I do not understand about my pain, Catherine. If I had to choose never to have known Andrea or to have known her for one brief moment, I would have chosen to have known her and considered myself fortunate. Is it the unexpectedness that causes my grief?"

Catherine pulled her shawl up high enough to cover her

chin. "How is David?"

MaryAnne swallowed. "I do not know how David feels, he says nothing. But I see the gray in his eyes and it frightens me. It is the gray of hate, not grief." She shook her head. "It is not just Andrea's life that was taken from us."

There was a moment of silence, then MaryAnne suddenly erupted in rage.

"Listen to me, Catherine! Our lives! My memories! My pain! It is all so selfish! One would think that it is I who had died! Am I so consumed with myself and my own agony that I do not even know if I am mourning for what my little girl has lost..." She stopped, her mouth quivering beyond her ability to speak, and lifted her hand to her face. "Or... or what I have lost?"

Catherine closed her eyes tightly.

"The wretched fool that I am. Such a selfish, pitiful..."

Catherine grabbed MaryAnne's shoulders and pulled her into her arms. Tears streaked down both women's cheeks. "MaryAnne, no! Do not speak such! In what have you done wrong? Did not the mother of our Lord weep at the foot of his cross?!" Catherine pulled MaryAnne's head into her breast and bowed over her, kissing the crown of her head. She wept as MaryAnne sobbed helplessly.

"Oh, Catherine, my arms feel so empty."

☙☙

The sexton pulled the horse's head back, and the horse plodded forward. When David was alone, he slowly approached the stone monument. He glanced at its inscription. Our Little Angel. He knelt down on one knee before it. In a serene voice he said, "I've got to tell you something, honey. I am letting you go. I once thought that to release the pain was a type of betrayal. I now know the opposite is true–that the greatest gift I can give to you is to free you from the burden of my grief. If life is so precious that I mourned the loss of yours, how wrong to throw away mine. I wonder if the loss of my life has caused you the same pain that the loss of yours caused me." He stopped, glanced up to the angel, then dropped his head again. "I know how much you loved your mother. I promise you that I will not close my heart to her again." He looked around the cemetery, and the glare of the yard forced him to squint. "That's all I wanted to say." He closed his eyes for a moment, then rose and walked home.

THE LETTER

☙❧

"He went back to Chicago to find you."

A strange, sad smile lit her lips. "They think I'm a ghost, in Chicago. I have read that I haunt a theater there." She spoke the words with peculiar indifference. "Tell me about my son."

"He was loving and strong and loyal."

"Everything I am not."

MaryAnne just stared at the wretched woman. "How long have you been here? In the valley?"

"Months," she answered tersely.

"Why didn't you come to see David?"

The woman didn't answer, but suddenly glanced from side to side as if someone had joined them. "You pity me, perhaps. Or maybe hate me."

"Yes, I pity you. For what you traded away. For what you might have known. But I do not hate you."

"You wondered that I was a ghost?"

"I was told you had died," MaryAnne said.

"I am dead to all I have known. To everyone I have known. I roam this world in regret of all that might have been. Dead or not, I am a ghost. I never jumped from that bridge. Looking out over that black water..." She paused as if the very memory held terror still. "It should be of no surprise to anyone. My whole life I never fulfilled any promise. Even my dying. It is my curse, to live to lose my son twice." She suddenly stirred from her own mumbling. "I did not come to mourn my son. I lost him a lifetime ago. I came to mourn my choices. And meet one prom-

85

ise." Rose looked down at the offering she had left on his marker–a wooden toy carousel.

MaryAnne sniffed and brushed at her cheek, and the woman abruptly said, "You haven't the right to sorrow. You have had so much."

The words enraged MaryAnne. "So much to have lost. Everything I held dear is now only a memory."

"Memories are what we trade our mortality for. What I would do for just memories."

"Even when they bring such pain?"

Fresh tears fell down MaryAnne's cheek, but the woman only glared at her. Her hard countenance revealed no sympathy. "There are things worse than pain."

To her own surprise, MaryAnne's heart welled, no longer for herself, but for the austere soul of this woman. Unexpectedly, a single tear fell down the hard woman's cheek, and it rolled slowly like a drop of rain on cracked, baked desert clay. "Everyone dies. You have lived. You shan't ask for more."

THE LETTER

ʊʊ

"Truth is, won't be much longer when no one need fret over me."

"Don't talk that way."

"Didn't mean no offense by it. Just, man knows when his time's a comin'. Somethin' inside like a clock windin' down."

"I am not one to frequent cemeteries," Catherine rejoined. "In my mind or otherwise. Just foolishness, talking about death."

"I ain't got no problem with dyin', Miss Catherine, it's one of life's simpler things. Like nightfall, it don't require no decision." He paused for Catherine's reprimand, but she said nothing. "Just as well. What use's a horologist that can't see? Been my philosophy that if life ain't useful it ain't nothing. I met people still breathin' that been dead going on twenty years or more. Only difference between them and the stone-cold is a headstone and six feet of dirt."

THE LETTER

ᏋᏋ

"All that death requires of us is to forsake the future."

THE LOCKET

ᏋᏋ

"We stand here encompassed by winter: the barren trees with their fallen leaves, the silent riverbed. Nothing is more certain in life or in nature than death. We accept it as the way of things. Perhaps we are able because we have faith in spring. Yet somehow it seems different to us when death comes early. Much as we might bemoan an early winter, we feel robbed of something due. We feel cheated. Sometimes we rage. And sometimes we blame. And, in doing so, we say to God, 'My will be done, not Thine,' and we forget about the promise of spring." He glanced at Quaye. "In the cold of our soul's winter, we bury our hearts. and then we wonder why it is dark and why we feel so alone. And we risk spending so much of our lives occupied with our loss and what we have not, that we forget the beauty of what is and what we have still. And this is sometimes the greater loss."

He looked at Quaye. "This I know. There are more ways to lose a child than death. Perhaps those who lose a childhood to death are more fortunate than those who let the chalice of childhood slip from their grasp without ever drinking of it."

THE LOOKING GLASS

☙

I have seen trees die, large hale trees green of leaf and limb whose roots, for no discernable reason, have simply perished and brought down with them the life they once nurtured. I suppose it was somewhere between Thomas's home and the Arcadia that Esther decided to die–or, more accurately, that she was through living.

THE LOCKET

ᏰᎧᎱ

Lawrence frowned. "Don't rightly know what to reckon of it all. S'pose there is a heaven, I wanna know what kinda heaven it be. Is it a heaven for white folks? Or is it a different heaven for colored folk and white folk? What you make of it?"

David shrugged. "I am not an expert. I have only been to church on a few occasions. It seems to me that people who spend their lives dreaming about the gold-paved streets and heavenly mansions of the next life are no different than those who waste their time dreaming about it in this life. Only with a poorer sense of timing."

Lawrence responded in a low, rumbling laughter reserved for when he found something particularly amusing. He clenched down on his pipe. "Never thought of it that way," he replied.

"The way I see it, it's not about what you are going to get, it's about what you become. Divinity is doing what is right because your heart says it's right. And if that puts you on the wrong side of the pearly gates, seems you would be better off on the outside."

TIMEPIECE

෨෬

"I believe there are special lakes in hell reserved for people who prey on the defenseless."

"Then you believe in hell," she said.

"It's easier to believe in than heaven."

"I believe in hell. And in heaven. But I think they're the same place."

"How is that?"

"I believe death wakens us the the consequences of our actions–to feel the sorrow or joy we have caused in our lifetime. The location is irrelevant."

THE LOCKET

ତଡ଼

"I wonder if, in some unseen realm, MaryAnne was watching and was pleased that I had learned her lesson. That some things, like a parent's love, do last forever in a time and place where all broken hearts will forever be made whole. And if, in the silent vastness of a mysterious universe, or in the quietness of men's hearts, there is such a place as heaven, then it couldn't be anything more than that."

TIMEPIECE

ତଡ଼

On GOD

There are those who find God in the order of the universe–evidenced in elements as small as atomic nuclei to forces as massive as the cosmic energy that holds galaxies at bay. From Galileo to Einstein to Hawking, the great minds have wondered at the creator of such order; the balance of energy to prescribed laws and constants. While mathematics of the universe may connote the existence of a supreme being, to me it is that which *defies* math's probabilities–the impossibility of two objects colliding in an infinite void to indelibly alter each other's eternal course. In this there is divinity and an unseen hand.

Through the course of my own life I have come to believe that life is not gifted by the sweep of a clock's hand or the change of the season, but rather, experientially, each experience laid upon the previous, delivering us to a loftier plane. Perhaps this best describes my concept of God–the architect of that ascent and the divine, unseen wind that propels us through the uncharted waters of our own destiny. But salvation, spiritual or otherwise, is not a solitary matter and along such journeys there are companions placed along our travels and travails, fellow sojourners who forever alter our paths and sometimes carry us when we are too weary to carry ourselves.

THE LOOKING GLASS

"So, Murrow, you'll be losing your daughter twice," the doctor said jovially.

Dr. Murrow did not find the observation amusing and his skin tightened over his cheeks. He looked down at me, and then suddenly smiled maliciously. His voice boomed. "Ginny asked me to talk to these kids about how foolish it would be to get married so young, so I asked Michael how he plans to pay the rent. 'God will provide,' he said. So I asked him how he plans to put food on the table. 'God will provide,' he said again. I went back and told Ginny that the bad news is that our daughter is going to be homeless and hungry. The good news is that her boyfriend thinks I'm God."

THE LOCKET

☙❧

Dierdre looked suddenly thoughtful. "Sometimes I wish that I were more religious. I frequently think about God, but I do not often attend church. I just want to go for the right reason–because I really believe it, not because it is socially advantageous." She suddenly grinned. "Of course that's another check on my father's blacklist."

"I think you are more religious than you give yourself credit for."

"How so?"

"There is integrity to your belief. I have to believe that pleases God."

"I don't think so. I think God wants blind observance."

"I find it difficult to accept that God created rational beings and would want them to be marionettes."

"Then what about faith?"

"Faith is misunderstood. It is treated as an end when, in fact, it is really a beginning."

"What do you mean?"

"It is a state we cultivate to get us somewhere–a principle of action. Every gold mine ever dug was dug by faith."

"But not all gold mines have gold."

"True, but you don't know that until you turn a shovel. It is only foolish, if one keeps panning when there is nothing there."

"I don't understand why faith is required at all. Why

doesn't God just appear to everyone and tell them what He wants them to do?"

"Then we would become marionettes. We would do things because of the promise of reward or the threat of punishment, not because they are intrinsically good or noble. Our actions would change, but our hearts wouldn't. The truth is, in this life, cause and effect are often disjointed. Sometimes very bad things happen to very good people–sometimes for doing the right thing." At the statement David paused. "...like with Andrea."

"Still, there is too much confusion. I think it would make sense for God to appeal more to the senses."

"I have come to the conclusion that if the one universal truth of existence is the unknowing, then there must be something in the unknowing. I believe that's what life is about–to learn what it is about. And, to the level we apply ourselves to learning this, we evolve."

"Evolve to what?"

"Hopefully, to a state closer to God."

"How does religion fit into your theory?"

"It is part of that evolution. Religion, in a way, is like a clock. I used to have more than a hundred of them. I could tell you where every one of them came from, what company made them, sometimes even how. Yet, I am the first to admit that I do not comprehend time. The things that this German scientist, Einstein, talks about may only be the first real glimpse of our understanding of time." He lifted his pocket watch and unclasped the shell that protected its crystal. "But I can read a clock. In the same way I cannot comprehend God or the magnitude of power that could create an infinite universe, let alone the human mind. So if religion can help me to understand that being, then I am better off. As long as I do not confuse the clock for the time."

THE LETTER

☙❧

ON BELONGING

David met Lawrence through the purchase of a Black Forest cuckoo clock and instantly liked the man. There was a calmness in his motion; the temperament of one suited to repair the intricate. "Slow hands," David called it. But there was more. There was something comfortable in his manner that reminded David of earlier days. Growing up in the womb of the Eureka mine, David had worked and lived with black men, listened to their stories of injustices and enjoyed their company. In the depth of a mine, all men were black, and he had learned to appreciate people for their souls. The two men spent hours talking about clocks, California, and the cavalry.

Though both were fascinated by clocks, they were so for vastly different reasons. Where David saw immortality in the perpetual motion of the clock's function, Lawrence was fascinated by the mechanism itself, and for hours on end, he would lose himself in a brass clockwork society—a perfect miniature world where all parts moved according to function. And every member had a place.

TIMEPIECE

༖

The bricked patio was visible from the spacious room, encircled by the garden and a pond lined by a wrought iron fence and weathered garden statuary. Dierdre walked up beside him.

"Most of my parents' social functions are held out on the patio. There used to be swans."

"What happened to them?"

"My mother was hosting a campaign fund raiser for an alderman and was standing by the pond when one of the birds took after her. You wouldn't think a woman could move so quickly in a long gown and heels. The bird only stopped chase when one of the guests headed it off with a pair of salad tongs. Everyone who is anyone was there, and to my mother's mortification, at every social function since then someone has recalled the incident."

David laughed. "What became of the swan?"

"Mother would have had the thing roasted if my father had allowed it. He sent them off to a park somewhere in the city. Mean birds, swans. Beautiful things are often mean."

THE LETTER

∞

"They sacrificed their love for me."

"Your father was a noble man."

Sophia looked at David thoughtfully. "There are people with fair complexions and beautiful faces with spirits as twisted and gnarled as burr oak. My parents were the comely ones. The ones with beautiful souls."

THE LETTER

ꝏ

Those with the softest hearts build the hardest shells.

THE LOCKET

ꝏ

"Mr. Parkin, you can't go buryin' a Negro up in this part of the cemetery."

"Why not?"

"It's against the law burying a Negro with white folk. Coloreds have their own place."

"Where?"

"In the colored section. On the south side."

David knew the place, a crowded, overgrown weed patch contained by a black spear fence.

"This is a city cemetery. He should be buried here."

The sexton's face twisted. "There'll be complaints."

David glanced around the graveyard. "You get complaints from them in here?"

"Well, no, but. . ." he stammered, "the folks that come."

"It's not their home."

"Maybe not, but it's against the law."

David pondered the dilemma. "Where does the law actually take offense in burying a Negro near a white man?"

"Don't follow ya."

"What part of the Negro is offensive?"

"What part?"

"It couldn't be the hair, my hair is dark. In fact, my hair is darker than Lawrence's since he grayed. Couldn't be his eyes. Is it just the skin? Having black flesh?"

"Stands to reason. That's what makes a Negro, ain't it?"

"It is?"

The old man didn't answer.

"Tell me, how long before the skin starts to decay?"

The macabre question surprised the man. "How long? Get 'm in the ground, suppose five weeks. Let 'm sit around in the sun a few days and might be only three."

"Then these folks buried here aren't really white."

"Well, most of 'em..."

"I don't see where we have a problem here." David counted out bills from a stack of currency and handed it to the man. "See to my request."

THE LETTER

☙❧

"It didn't go quite how I expected it would, but I got my answers. Turns out that my mother never amounted to anything, and she ended up jumping from a bridge. My whole life I have felt like I needed to talk to her, to ask her why she left me. But I realized that what I really wanted to know is why I wasn't worthy of her love. That is something she couldn't have answered, because I was worthy of her love, whether she gave it to me or not. Every child is worthy of love." David sniffed, then rubbed his nose. "In a way, she was also looking for love. She thought she could find it in the applause of an audience. But what good is the love of strangers if your life is of no value to your own child?"

THE LETTER

☙

"No one, except Lawrence, ever called my mother beautiful. My mother was a beautiful woman, David, but not because society would bestow the title. She was beautiful because her spirit was beautiful. The world shunned her as disfigured and hideous. Most of my mother's face was covered with a cruel birthmark. I don't think Lawrence could see the blemish. In a way he was the same as her, they were both victims of their skin."

"What a shock this must all be to you."

"My mother didn't want anyone to know that I was half Negro–she even hid it from me. She prayed that I would be fair-skinned. A 'pe-ola.' She straightened my hair with pomade and a curling iron." She smiled sadly. "Imagine my surprise when I found out that my father was a Negro–that I am a Negro. Every belief that I accepted from society I now have to atone for with my own self-perspective. I do not feel any different than I did yesterday. I do not look or speak or think differently. But today I am a Negro. Am I to think less of myself?

"Mama worked hard to teach me that people are people and not to be judged by their appearances. I once thought that she taught me this because of her own flesh, her own mark. It wasn't so. It was to save me. She taught me so that I would not hate myself someday."

"Your mother was wise."

Sophia reflected on her mother and smiled distantly. "She was a good woman. She always knew the right thing to say."

THE LETTER

ᛞᚷ

"If Jak can convince you that your existence was worthless to the one who gave you life, he will win the battle in subjecting you to his whim. Our false beliefs can be a chain to our souls. Only if we hold on to who we truly are can we be free. The danger is in the forgetting."

Quaye looked shaken. "Those were my father's last words to me. If I would remember who I am..."

"I can't know what went through your father's mind as he gave you up. Maybe your father knew what kind of man Jak was, maybe he didn't, but it is likely that he knew that there was no other way to help you. So he did what he had to do to give you a chance at life."

Hunter looked out into the starry night. "We do not see things in this life as they really are—only as we believe they are. It is as written in The Bible, we see through a glass darkly—but no glass is so dark, I think, as the looking glass in which we view ourselves."

"A looking glass cannot lie," Quaye said. "It is just polished glass."

"It is not the looking glass that lies. Nowhere does man err more greatly than when he looks to see the reality of who he is."

"And who are we?"

Hunter looked into her soft eyes. "We are worthy, Quaye. Worthy of life. Worthy of love. Worthy of kindness and gentleness. We are not some mistake of God or nature."

Quaye did not want Hunter to see her cry. She bowed her head, pulling the blanket above her chin.

"Until you can see yourself worthy of love, you will forever be chained. Not by Jak, or any man, but by your own perception."

THE LOOKING GLASS

೮೮

"Hello, Leroy."

"Need to talk with you," he said tensely.

David motioned to a chair. "Of course. Sit down."

Leroy walked to the chair but stood behind it, nervously swaying from foot to foot.

"'Bout what you said earlier. 'Bout the two percent and all. We may be Okies, but I been around some. That's just hooey."

David leaned back in his seat, carefully studying the boy's expression.

"I want to know why you'd go givin' us two hunderd dollars we both know you ain't never gonna see again."

"Why do you think?"

"Don't know what to think. My pap's just a farmer. He don't know 'bout finance and stuff. He still don't know how it was them bankers came and took our land. I gotta tell him like it is, Mister Parkin. Gotta tell him somethin' ain't right."

"I don't think you should do that, Leroy."

Leroy answered defensively, "Why shouldn't I?"

"People like your father are the mortar that holds this world together. And it's their dignity that holds them together. Say you go on and tell him that it's really just charity I'm offering. Then, if he takes the money he loses himself. Or, if he decides to decline the money, he loses his family. Either way a good man loses. You take his dignity from him and you're as damned a fool as the bankers."

Leroy could not reply.

"Your father's not just a farmer. He's not just anything. A man's worth isn't measured by a bank register or a diploma, Leroy. It's about integrity. You remember that."

The boy looked embarrassed. "I'm sorry, Mister Parkin."

"It's all right, Leroy. You just care about your folks. There's not a thing wrong with that."

Leroy nodded thoughtfully as he quietly walked out of the room.

THE LETTER

⯌

"David?"

He turned toward her.

"What did he say?"

"He said there is nothing they can do. . ."

MaryAnne quietly looked down, cradling her forehead in her hands, then look back up at David. "What are you doing?"

His eyes were granite. "What needs to be done."

MaryAnne walked over next to him. "David?"

He would not look at her.

MaryAnne knelt down before him and wrapped her arms around his legs and began to cry. A minute later, she looked up, her eyes filled with pleading.

"They killed our daughter," he said coldly.

"The men who killed our little girl were full of hate and vengeance and sickness. Will we become as they?"

David paused for a moment, then looked down at his wife.

"It is the price of justice."

"Such a price, David! How much more must we pay?!" She took a deep breath, her chin quivered. "Haven't we paid enough already?"

"You would have me forget what they have done?"

MaryAnne gasped. "How could we forget what they have done? We can never forget." She raised her head and as she did their eyes met. "But we can forgive. We must forgive. It is all that we have left of her."

"Forgive?" David asked softly. He broke her grasp and walked to the other side of the room. "Forgive?!" he shouted incredulously. "They murdered our daughter!"

MaryAnne sobbed into her hands, then, without looking up, spoke in a voice feeble with grief. "If this is life, exchanging hate for hate, it is not worth living. Vengeance will not bring her back to us. Forgiveness has nothing to do with them, David. It has to do with us. It has to do with who we are and who we will become." She looked up, her eyes drowned in tears. "It has to do with how we want to remember our daughter."

Her words trailed off in a pleading silence. David stared at his wife. "Who we will become," he repeated softly. He leaned the rifle against the cabinet, then returned and knelt by MaryAnne, wrapping his arms around her as she wept into his chest.

"David, I cannot imagine feeling any joy again in this life. It seems that all I can do is to ride the tide of the day's events. But I cannot bear to see any more hate. We must let it end here." She wiped her eyes with the palm of her hand. "I have already lost one of you to hate."

She placed her hand on his sleeve, gripping it tightly. David looked back over at the gun and as he did, she released her grasp. Her voice became soft, yet deliberate. "I cannot choose for you, David. It is your choice, not mine.

But if you will be taken by it, I ask that you promise me just one thing."

David looked into her eyes. They were red and swollen, but beautiful still.

"What would you have me promise, Mary?'

"That you will save one bullet for my heart."

TIMEPIECE

☼

"You were right. It is all that I have left of her. All my feelings and love for Andrea were in my heart–" he rubbed his eyes–"and hate kills the heart. Even broken ones."

TIMEPIECE

☼

"Indignation, righteous or otherwise, is a weapon. We must be cautious in its handling," she said, "for a weapon will kill the innocent just as dead as the guilty."

THE LOCKET

☼

"What was your father like?"

She sighed. "Oh, he was a timid man. Miners used to say he looked like an emaciated version of Herbert Hoover. I suppose he was just about as popular. With my mother gone we traveled constantly, always chasing an easy dollar. He was a fool and a schemer, but he was always scheming on my behalf. He never forsook that responsibility for me. Now that I'm old, I understand that, and I love him for that. Not that I'm any wiser, just that old age lends perspective. And that leads to forgiveness."

"I couldn't say that about my father," I said tersely. "I will never forgive him."

She looked disturbed by my comment. "You say that as if forgiveness was a gift you were giving to him."

"Isn't it?"

"Your father is dead. What could forgiveness possibly profit him?"

I could not answer her question. "You think that I should forgive my father?" I asked incredulously.

"You must forgive him if you are ever to be free of him. We are chained to that which we do not forgive."

"I'm not chained to my father," I asserted.

"Far more than you know, apparently. Imagine a ship trying to set sail while towing an anchor. Cutting free is not a gift to the anchor. You must release that burden, not because the anchor is worthy, but because the ship is."

I thought of my father and immediately felt the blackness

that enveloped all memory of him. "I don't know if I could forgive him for abandoning us. Even if I wanted to."

"Anyone can forgive if they will make the decision to. It may not come all at once, as resentment is a habit and must be coaxed from the heart. But with time it will come. You must pray for it. You must pray for the unforgiven."

"It would seem that forgiving him would be a betrayal of my mother."

"Would it please your mother to know that you were filled with hate?"

The question left me speechless.

"Sometimes forgiveness comes with understanding."

THE LOCKET

☙☞

"There are those who clutch to resentment like it were a treasure of great worth. This is foolishness. The question to be asked is not how badly we were wronged, but what are we profited by our unforgiveness?"

THE LOCKET

☙☞

There were things about my mother I had never understood. Such as why she had kept my father's name. I had assumed that, like most of the unpleasantnesses of her life, it was something that she had done for me. To spare me any embarrassment that it might engender. But there was something else about my mother that was even more peculiar.

She wept when she learned of my father's death.

It was suddenly clear to me why. My mother had kept his name because she had never stopped loving him. As inconceivable as that seemed to me, there was something about him that was still worthy of her love and she not only seemed to love him after he abandoned us but she loved him more so.

At that moment I understood that Esther had been right, not just about me but about my father as well. That my father never loved alcohol. It owned him, but he did not love it. But he did, perhaps, love us. In his sober moments he would sometimes weep bitterly for the pain he caused my mother and me. I remembered something that I rarely allowed to enter my mind, lest I allow mercy to enter with it and plead in his behalf. Just before my father left us, he came to me and begged me for my forgiveness—an appeal I responded to with hatred and rejection. I remember his face as he left. It was twisted in anguish, but not condemnation. He understood, he said; he deserved no less. And then he was gone.

Esther was right. My father had never stopped loving us. But he knew from years of failure that he couldn't free himself from the chains of his addiction, so he sacrificed his own heart to set us free. He died alone.

For the first time in my life I wept not for the pain my father had caused us but the pain of his life. I wept for him. And in some mystical, miraculous way, in those tears I found something that had eluded me since I was old enough to understand its absence from my life. I found peace. As elusive as it had seemed, it had been where it had always been, concealed behind a door of forgiveness.

I looked again at the name on the grave and I was certain of what forgiveness required of me. To set aside the known shackles of the past for the untested wings of the future. I was to protect and honor my father's name.

THE LOCKET

✺

ON HOPE

Hope is a rare gift that, if we are lucky, comes to us with the power to heal our lives. I've come to know that the deepest sense of hope often springs from the hardest lessons in life. It is in the darkest skies that stars are best seen—perhaps it is divine irony that within the darkest moments we are capable of revealing the greatest light, demonstrating what is best with humanity.

TIMEPIECE

ॐ

"I don't mourn for my father," Sophia said as they left the cemetery. She wiped her eyes with a moist handkerchief.

"I believe that my parents are finally together in a place where love knows no color. . . nor deformity. But there are things I regret not being able to ask him. I understand the danger that his relationship with my mother posed. But his abandonment was so complete. I will always wonder why he never came to me."

"I can't understand it," David replied. "He was so close to our little girl. I am still astonished that after all these years he never told me he had a daughter."

"I know this will sound terrible, but I have wondered if his fear of being discovered was just greater than his love for me."

David turned from the road, glancing sternly into Sophia's eyes. "Lawrence was no coward. It's just not so."

"I would almost rather hear that he was. Then, at least, I would know why. The unknowing is worse than any truth."

David's countenance relaxed. "You and I have much in common, Sophia. In a sense, your journey is the same as mine. My own mother abandoned me when I was a child. I also went out to find my mother in search of answers. But she had already died."

"What did you hope to find?"

"Understanding of why I was not worthy of her."

"Then your journey was also a failure."

"Not at all. I brought back what I needed."

"What did you learn?"

"To leave the past behind. The answers are not in the past. Healing comes from purpose and purpose resides in our hope of the future."

THE LETTER

&.

ON KEEPING DIARIES

I find myself astonished at mankind's persistent yet vain attempts to escape the certainty of oblivion; expressed in nothing less than the ancient pyramids and by nothing more than a stick in a child's hand, etching a name into a freshly poured sidewalk. To leave our mark in the unset concrete of time–something to say we existed.

Perhaps this is what drives our species to diaries, that some unborn generation may know we once loved, hated, worried, and laughed. And what is there to this? Maybe nothing more than poetic gesture, for diaries die with their authors–or so I once believed. I have learned there is more to the exercise. For as we chronicle our lives and the circumstances that surround them, our perspectives and stretching rationales, what lies before us is our own reflection. It is the glance in the mirror that is of value. These are my words on the matter and I leave it at this–if we write but one book in life, let it be our autobiography.

TIMEPIECE

&ა:

Jenna looked back down at the timepiece.

"Nineteen years ago, MaryAnne asked me to give this to you the night before your wedding. It was her most prized possession."

Jenna shook her head in astonishment. "She wanted me to have it?"

I nodded. "MaryAnne was a good giver of gifts," I said.

She draped the gold watch back in its case, set it on her nightstand, then sighed. "So are you, Dad."

I smiled.

"Dad?"

"Yes?"

She turned away and I noticed that her chin quivered as she struggled to speak. As she turned back, her tear-filled eyes met mine. "So, how do you thank someone for a life?"

I wiped a tear from my cheek as I stared back into my daughter's beautiful eyes. Then, in that bittersweet moment, I understood MaryAnne's words of the gift. The great gift. The meaning of the timepiece.

"You give it back, Jenna. You give it back." I took my girl in my arms and held her tightly to my chest. My heart, bathed in fond memory, ached in the sweet pain of separation. This is what it meant to be a father–had always meant. To know that one day I would turn around and my little girl would be gone. Finally, reluctantly, I released her and leaned back, looking down into her angelic face. It was time. Time for the cycle to begin anew.

"It's late, sweetheart. You have a big day tomorrow." I leaned over and kissed her tenderly on the cheek. "Good-bye honey."

It was good-bye. To an era. A time never to be returned to. Her eyes shone with sadness and love. "Good-bye, Daddy."

The silence of the snow-shrouded evening enveloped the moment and time seemed to stand still for just a moment. For just us.

I took a deep breath, rose from the side of her bed, and with one last embrace walked from her room. I descended the stairway with a new lightness of understanding. I understood what MaryAnne had meant by the gift. The gift Jenna had given me had been life. That the very breath I had once given to her had come back to me in an infinite return of joy and life and meaning.

In the dimly lit entrance below, the grandfather clock struck once for the hour, and I paused momentarily at the base of the stairway to look into its time-faded face as, perhaps, MaryAnne and David had done so many years before.

This relic will outlive us all, I thought, just as it had out-lived generations before us. For within its cotillion of levers and cogs and gears, there was still time. Time to outlive all things human. Yet, in my heart, something told me otherwise. For perhaps there was some quality about love that sprang eternal—that a love like MaryAnne's, and like mine, could last forever.

Not could. Would. This was the message of the timepiece. To let go of this world and aspire to something far nobler in a realm that regards no boundaries of time.

TIMEPIECE

☙❧

I sat down in the rocker in front of the illuminated Christmas tree and lay my head in my hands. Somewhere between the angel and Mary's house I had figured it out. The first gift of Christmas. It just came. It came to my heart. The first gift of Christmas was love. A parent's love. Pure as the first snows of Christmas. For God so loved His children that He sent His son, that we might someday return to Him. I understood what Mary had been trying to teach me. I stood up and walked up the stairs where my little girl lay sleeping. I picked up her warm little body and, cradling her tightly in my arms, brought her back down to the den. My tears fell on her hair. My little girl. My precious little girl. How foolish I had been to let her childhood, her fleeting, precious childhood slip away. Forever. In my young mind everything was so permanent and lasting. My little girl would be my little girl forever. But time would prove me wrong. Someday she'd grow up. Someday she'd be gone and I would be left with the memory of giggles and secrets I might have known.

Jenna took a deep breath and snuggled close for warmth. I held her little body tightly against mine. This is what it meant to be a father, to know that one day I would turn around and my little girl would be gone. To look upon the sleeping little girl and to die a little inside. For one precious, fleeting moment, to hold the child in my arms, and would that time stood still.

But none of that mattered now. Not now. Not tonight. Tonight Jenna was mine and no one could take this Christmas Eve away from me but me. How wise Mary had been. Mary, who knew the pain of a father sending his son away on that first Christmas morn, knowing full well the path that lay ahead. Mary understood Christmas. The tears in the Bible showed that. Mary loved with the pure, sweet love of a mother, a love so deep that it becomes the allegory for all other love. She knew that in my quest for success in this world I had been trading diamonds for stones. She knew, and she loved me enough to help me see. Mary had given me the greatest gift of Christmas. My daughter's childhood.

THE CHRISTMAS BOX

ഗ

From the inlaid jade-and-coral jewelry boxes of the Orient to the utilitarian salt boxes of the Pennsylvania Dutch, the allure of the box has transcended all cultural and geographical boundaries of the world. The cigar box, the snuff box, the cash box, jewelry boxes more ornate than the treasure they hold, the ice box, and the candle box. Trunks, long rectangular boxes covered with cowhide, stretched taut, and pounded with brass studs to a wooden frame. Oak boxes, sterling boxes, to the delight of the women, hat boxes and shoe boxes, and to the delight of all enslaved by a sweet tooth, candy boxes. The human life cycle no less than evolves around the box; from the open-topped box called a bassinet, to the pine box we call a coffin, the box is our past and, just as assuredly, our future. It should not surprise us then that the lowly box plays such a significant role in the first Christmas story. For Christmas began in a humble, hay-filled box of splintered wood. The Magi, wise men who had traveled far to see the infant king, laid treasure-filled boxes at the feet of that holy child. And in the end, when He had ransomed our sins with His blood, the Lord of Christmas was laid down in a box of stone. How fitting that each Christmas season brightly wrapped boxes skirt the pine boughs of Christmas trees around the world. And more fitting that I learned of Christmas through a Christmas Box.

THE CHRISTMAS BOX

☙❧

RICHARD PAUL EVANS TITLES

The Christmas Box
Timepiece
The Letter
The Locket
The Looking Glass
The Carousel

The Christmas Candle: *A children's book*
The Dance: *A children's book*
The Spyglass: *A children's book*

The First Gift of Christmas: *A book of poetry*
The Baby Grand: *A book card*
The Quotable Evans

Watch for future titles

Please send correspondence to:
Richard Paul Evans
P.O. Box 1416
Salt Lake City, UT 84110

Or visit his website: **www.richardpaulevans.com**

PERSONAL REFERENCE

PG #	TOPIC/NOTES
....	....
....	....
....	....
....	....
....	....
....	....
....	....
....	....
....	....
....	....
....	....
....	....
....	....
....	....
....	....
....	....
....	....
....	....
....	....
....	....
....	....
....	....
....	....
....	....
....	....
....	....
....	....
....	....

PERSONAL REFERENCE

PG #	TOPIC/NOTES
....	....
....	....
....	....
....	....
....	....
....	....
....	....
....	....
....	....
....	....
....	....
....	....
....	....
....	....
....	....
....	....
....	....
....	....
....	....
....	....
....	....
....	....
....	....
....	....
....	....
....	....
....	....

$\mathcal{P}$ERSONAL REFERENCE

PG #	TOPIC/NOTES
....	....
....	....
....	....
....	....
....	....
....	....
....	....
....	....
....	....
....	....
....	....
....	....
....	....
....	....
....	....
....	....
....	....
....	....
....	....
....	....
....	....
....	....
....	....
....	....
....	....
....	....